Bria

Confident in Christ We Pray
Daily Prayer for Lent and Easter

YEAR C

columba

First published in 2007 by
THE COLUMBA PRESS
55a Spruce Avenue, Stillorgan Industrial Park,
Blackrock, Co Dublin, Ireland

Designed by Bill Bolger
Origination by The Columba Press
Printed in Ireland by ColourBooks Ltd, Dublin

ISBN 978 1 85607 564 0

Copyright © 2006, Brian Mayne

Contents

Introduction	5
Ash Wednesday and days following	7
First Week of Lent	12
Second Week of Lent	18
Third Week of Lent	24
Fourth Week of Lent	30
Fifth Week of Lent	37
Holy Week: Monday, Tuesday and Wednesday	43
Holy Week: Maundy Thursday, Good Friday and Holy Saturday	50
First Week of Easter	57
Second Week of Easter	63
Third Week of Easter	68
Fourth Week of Easter	75
Fifth Week of Easter	81
Sixth Week of Easter	87
The Ascension Day	92
Days between the Ascension Day and Pentecost	97
The Day of Pentecost	103
Acknowledgements	109

For
Elizabeth

Introduction

Confident in Christ, we pray completes the trilogy begun with *As we believe so we pray – daily prayer for Lent and Easter Year A* and continued with *Believing we pray* for Year B. It is offered as material for personal prayer in these seasons for Year C. It is constructed round the Sunday Gospels which, apart from the Second Sunday in Lent, are the same in both *Revised Common Lectionary* and *Ordo lectio missae*. This gives people in different denominations an opportunity to reflect together and pray together.

A scripture sentence sets the tone. This is followed by a prayer of penitence, drawn from various sources, some written for this book. I have again selected classical hymns suitable for each week. Psalmody is at the centre – a refrain is provided. Over the week this may be used before or after the psalm or before and after a verse or group of verses. Once again I have been able to use the listings of *Revised Common Lectionary Daily Readings* which was published in late 2005 by the Consultation on Common Texts. The compilers graciously allowed me permission to use these excerpts. To use these requires having a bible at hand. For Holy Week and the week of Easter Day I have used my own choices. Normally the Gospel passage of the week, or part of it, is also printed allowing for its extended use. (I have used another reading for two weeks where the Gospel in Year C is the same as that in Years A and B.)

A canticle offers a biblical response to our reading. Here, I have gone beyond the Church of Ireland *Book of Common Prayer* and included some of the canticles in *Common Worship – Daily Prayer* (2005).

Possible subjects are suggested for prayer and thanksgiving. Here one's own words however faltering are enough. This can be concluded with the Prayer Book Collect or other prayers. This year I have included some of the prayers from the CD of *Uniting in Prayer II* – the worship resource of the Uniting Church of Australia. I hope that these and other prayers from different parts of the world will enrich our praying. Finally, we pray the Lord's Prayer and a short 'ending' to send us on our way.

I hope that all who use this book will be find that their confidence in Christ, who suffered, died and rose for us, is strengthened and that the whole period of Lent and Easter will be a time of growth.

Brian Mayne
Saint Matthew's Day 2006

Ash Wednesday and days following

Preparation

A SENTENCE OF SCRIPTURE

Jesus said: 'Beware of practising your piety before others in order to be seen by them; for then you have no reward from your Father in heaven.' *Matthew 6: 1*

A PRAYER OF PENITENCE

Gracious God,
have mercy on us.
In your compassion forgive us our sins,
known and unknown,
things done and things left undone.
Uphold us with your Spirit
so that we may live and serve you in newness of life,
to the honour and glory of your holy name;
through Jesus Christ our Lord. Amen.

Sundays and Seasons

HYMN

Lord Jesu, think on me,
with many a care oppressed;
let me thy loving servant be,
and taste thy promised rest.

Lord Jesu, think on me,
nor let me go astray;
through darkness and perplexity
point thou the heavenly way.

Lord Jesu, think on me,
that, when the flood is past,
I may the eternal brightness see,
and share thy joy at last. *Bishop Synesius, 373-430*

The Word of God

PSALM 51: 1-5

Turn your face from my sins ▪
and blot out all my misdeeds.

1 Have mercy on me, O God, in your great goodness; ▪
   according to the abundance of your compassion
   blot out my offences.
2 Wash me thoroughly from my wickedness ▪
   and cleanse me from my sin.
3 For I acknowledge my faults ▪
   and my sin is ever before me.
4 Against you only have I sinned ▪
   and done what is evil in your sight,
5 So that you are justified in your sentence ▪
   and righteous in your judgement.

A BIBLE READING

GOD'S CALL AND PROMISE

Ash Wednesday	*Joel 2: 1-2, 12-17*
Thursday	*Acts 7: 30-34*
Friday	*Exodus 6: 2-13*
Saturday	*John 12: 27-36*

or

Blow the trumpet in Zion;
   sound the alarm on my holy mountain!
Let all the inhabitants of the land tremble,
   for the day of the Lord is coming, it is near –

a day of darkness and gloom,
   a day of clouds and thick darkness!
Yet even now, says the Lord,
   return to me with all your heart,
with fasting, with weeping, and with mourning;
   rend your hearts and not your clothing.
Return to the Lord, your God,
   for he is gracious and merciful,
slow to anger, and abounding in steadfast love,
   and relents from punishing.
Blow the trumpet in Zion;
   sanctify a fast;
call a solemn assembly;
   gather the people.

Joel 2: 1, 12-13, 15

A CANTICLE

SAVIOUR OF THE WORLD

1 Jesus Saviour of the world,
    come to us in your mercy: ▪
  we look to you to save and help us.

2 By your cross and your life laid down,
    you set your people free: ▪
  we look to you to save and help us.

3 When they were ready to perish
    you saved your disciples: ▪
  we look to you to come to our help.

4 In the greatness of your mercy
    loose us from our chains: ▪
  forgive the sins of all your people.

5 Make yourself known as our Saviour
    and mighty Deliverer: ▪
  save and help us that we may praise you.

6 Come now and dwell with us Lord Christ Jesus, ▪
   hear our prayer and be with us always.
7 And when you come in your glory ▪
   make us to be one with you
   and to share the life of your kingdom. Amen.

Prayer

INTERCESSIONS AND THANKSGIVINGS

Pray to grow in confident faith during this season of Lent
   for all seeking to renew their experience of God's love at
   this time,
   all who are indifferent to God's claims on their lives.
Give thanks for the assurance that Jesus understands
   human struggle against temptation,
   the assurance that God's mercy knows no limit,
   for all acts of compassion and kindness that reveal
   Christ's Spirit at work in the world.

THE COLLECT OF ASH WEDNESDAY

Almighty and everlasting God,
you hate nothing that you have made
and forgive the sins of all those who are penitent:
Create and make in us new and contrite hearts
that we, worthily lamenting our sins
and acknowledging our wretchedness,
may receive from you, the God of all mercy,
perfect remission and forgiveness;
through Jesus Christ our Lord. Amen.

or one of these prayers
Almighty and merciful God,
at this time you call your people to cleanse their hearts,
and prepare with joy to celebrate the mighty acts

by which you have brought our redemption:
as we mourn our sins which separate us from you
renew us with your grace,
that with all the choirs of angels
and with the faithful people of every time and place,
we may praise your name
and see the fulness of your glory;
through Jesus Christ our Lord. Amen.

Holy God,
our lives are laid open before you:
Rescue us from the chaos of sin
and through the death of your Son
bring us healing and make us whole
in Jesus Christ our Lord. Amen. *Alternative Collects*

THE LORD'S PRAYER

AN ENDING

The grace and mercy of God,
who in Christ bears our burdens and saves us from sin,
be with us all. *Sundays and Seasons*

Ash Wednesday and the days following

The First Week of Lent

Preparation

A SENTENCE OF SCRIPTURE

Put your trust in God; for I will yet give him thanks,
who is the help of my countenance and my God.

Psalm 42: 14

A PRAYER OF PENITENCE

In the wilderness we find your grace:
you love us with everlasting love.

Lord, have mercy.

There is none but you to uphold our cause:
our sin cries out and our guilt is great.

Christ, have mercy.

Heal us, O Lord, and we shall be healed:
restore us and we shall know your joy

Lord, have mercy.

HYMN

Approach, my soul, the mercy-seat
where Jesus answers prayer;
there humbly fall before his feet,
for none can perish there.

Thy promise is my only plea,
with this I venture nigh;
thou callest burdened souls to thee,
and such, O Lord, am I.

Bowed down beneath a load of sin,
by Satan sorely pressed,
by war without, and fears within,
I come to thee for rest.

Be thou my shield and hiding place,
that, sheltered near thy side,
I may my fierce accuser face,
and tell him thou hast died.

O wondrous love, to bleed and die,
to bear the Cross and shame,
that guilty sinners, such as I,
might plead thy gracious Name!

John Newton, 1725-1807

The Word of God

PSALM 91: 1-8

I am with them in trouble ■
I will deliver them and bring them to honour

1 Whoever dwells in the shelter of the Most High ■
    and abides under the shadow of the Almighty,
2 Shall say to the Lord, 'My refuge and my stronghold, ■
    my God, in whom I put my trust.'
3 For he shall deliver you from the snare of the fowler ■
    and from the deadly pestilence.
4 He shall cover you with his wings
    and you shall be safe under his feathers; ■
    his faithfulness shall be your shield and buckler.
5 You shall not be afraid of any terror by night, ■
    nor of the arrow that flies by day;
6 Of the pestilence that stalks in darkness, ■
    nor of the sickness that destroys at noonday.

First Week of Lent

7 Though a thousand fall at your side
    and ten thousand at your right hand, ▪
  yet it shall not come near you.
8 Your eyes have only to behold ▪
  to see the reward of the wicked.

A BIBLE READING

TESTED

Monday	*1 Chronicles 21: 1-17*
Tuesday	*Zechariah 3: 1-10*
Wednesday	*Job 1: 1-22*

WHERE WE BELONG

Thursday	*Genesis 13: 17-18*
Friday	*Philippians 3: 17-20*
Saturday	*Matthew 23: 37-39*

or

Jesus, full of the Holy Spirit, returned from the Jordan and was led by the Spirit in the wilderness, where for forty days he was tempted by the devil. He ate nothing at all during those days, and when they were over, he was famished. The devil said to him, 'If you are the Son of God, command this stone to become a loaf of bread.' Jesus answered him, 'It is written, "One does not live by bread alone." '

Then the devil led him up and showed him in an instant all the kingdoms of the world. And the devil said to him, 'To you I will give their glory and all this authority; for it has been given over to me, and I give it to anyone I please. If you, then, will worship me, it will all be yours.' Jesus answered him, 'It is written, "Worship the Lord your God, and serve only him." '

Then the devil took him to Jerusalem, and placed

him on the pinnacle of the temple, saying to him, 'If you are the Son of God, throw yourself down from here, for it is written, "He will command his angels concerning you, to protect you", and "On their hands they will bear you up, so that you will not dash your foot against a stone."'

Jesus answered him, 'It is said, "Do not put the Lord your God to the test." ' When the devil had finished every test, he departed from him until an opportune time. *Luke 4: 1-13*

A CANTICLE

SONG OF MANASSEH
Manasseh 1a, 2, 4, 6, 7a, 7b, 9a, 9c, 11, 12, 14b, 15b

1 Lord almighty and God of our ancestors, ▪
   who made heaven and earth in all their glory:
2 All things tremble with awe at your presence, ▪
   before your great and mighty power.
3 Immeasurable and unsearchable is your promised mercy, ▪
   for you are God, Most High.
4 You are full of compassion, long-suffering and very merciful, ▪
   and you relent at human suffering.
5 O God, according to your great goodness, ▪
   you have promised forgiveness for repentance
     to those who have sinned against you.
6 The sins I have committed against you ▪
   are more in number than the sands of the sea.
7 I am not worthy to look up to the height of heaven, ▪
   because of the multitude of my iniquities.

First Week of Lent

8 And now I bend the knee of my heart before you, ▪
   imploring your kindness upon me.
9 I have sinned, O God, I have sinned, ▪
   and I acknowledge my transgressions.
10 Unworthy as I am, you will save me, ▪
   according to your great mercy.
11 For all the host of heaven sings your praise, ▪
   and your glory is for ever and ever.

Prayer

INTERCESSIONS AND THANKSGIVINGS

Pray for those who face the temptations of greed, power and pride,

   for those tempted to harm themselves, especially young people with low esteem for themselves,

   for those who seek to gain their ends by evil means.

Give thanks for the gifts God gives his people to enable them to resist the power of evil,

   for all the unselfish people whom God uses to help those otherwise lost to addiction,

   for all that sets people free from pain and fear.

THE COLLECT OF LENT 1

Almighty God,
whose Son Jesus Christ fasted forty days in the wilderness,
and was tempted as we are, yet without sin:
Give us grace to discipline ourselves
in obedience to your Spirit;
and, as you know our weakness,
so may we know your power to save;
through Jesus Christ our Lord. Amen.

or one of these prayers
Almighty God,
whose blessed Son was led by the Spirit to be tempted
   by Satan:
Come quickly to help us who are assaulted by many
   temptations;
and, as you know our weaknesses,
let each one find you mighty to save;
through Jesus Christ your Son, our Lord.

Lutheran Renewal

God,
you know better than we do
the temptations that will bring us down.
By your love protect us
from all foolish and corrupting desires;
for Jesus' sake.   *Prayer Book of New Zealand altd.*

THE LORD'S PRAYER

AN ENDING

Save us, O Lord, while waking
and guard us while sleeping,
that awake we may watch with Christ,
and asleep we may rest in peace.

The Second Week of Lent

Preparation

A SENTENCE OF SCRIPTURE

God did not send the Son into the world to condemn the world, but in order that the world might be saved through him. *John 3: 17*

A PRAYER OF PENITENCE

Almighty and most merciful Father;
we have erred and strayed from thy ways
    like lost sheep.
We have followed too much the devices and desires
    of our own hearts.
We have offended against thy holy laws.
We have left undone those things
    which we ought to have done;
and we have done those things
    which we ought not to have done;
and there is no health in us.
But thou, O Lord, have mercy upon us,
    miserable offenders.
Spare thou them, O God, that confess their faults.
Restore thou them that are penitent;
according to thy promises
    declared unto mankind in Christ Jesus our Lord.
And grant, O most merciful Father, for his sake;
that we may hereafter live a godly, righteous,
    and sober life,
to the glory of thy holy Name. Amen.

Lead, kindly Light, amid the encircling gloom,
lead thou me on;
the night is dark, and I am far from home,
lead thou me on.
Keep thou my feet, I do not ask to see
the distant scene, one step enough for me.

I was not ever thus, nor prayed that thou
shouldst lead me on;
I loved to choose and see my path, but now
lead thou me on.
I loved the garish day, and spite of fears,
pride ruled my will; remember not past years.

So long thy power hath blest me, sure it still
will lead me on
o'er moor and fen, o'er crag and torrent, till
the night is gone,
and with the morn those angel faces smile,
which I have loved long since and lost awhile.

John Henry Newman, 1808-87

The Word of God

PSALM 27: 1-8

Teach my your way, O Lord! ■
lead me on a level path.

1 The Lord is my light and my salvation;
    whom then shall I fear? ■
  The Lord is the strength of my life;
    of whom then shall I be afraid?
2 When the wicked, even my enemies and my foes,
    came upon me to eat up my flesh, ■
  they stumbled and fell.

3 Though a host encamp against me,
    my heart shall not be afraid, ▪
  and though there rise up war against me,
    yet will I put my trust in him.
4 One thing have I asked of the Lord
    and that alone I seek: ▪
  that I may dwell in the house of the Lord
    all the days of my life,
5 To behold the fair beauty of the Lord ▪
  and to seek his will in his temple.
6 For in the day of trouble he shall hide me
    in his shelter; ▪
  in the secret place of his dwelling shall he hide me
    and set me high upon a rock.
7 And now shall he lift up my head ▪
  above my enemies round about me;
8 Therefore will I offer in his dwelling
    an oblation with great gladness; ▪
  I will sing and make music to the Lord.

A BIBLE READING

THE WAY TO GOD

Monday	*Romans 4: 1-12*
Tuesday	*1 Corinthians 10: 1-13*
Wednesday	*Luke 13: 22-31*

RESPONSE

Thursday	*Revelation 2: 8-11*
Friday	*Revelation 3: 1-6*
Saturday	*Luke 6: 43-45*

or

At that very hour some Pharisees came and said to Jesus, 'Get away from here, for Herod wants to kill you.' He said to them, 'Go and tell that fox for me, "Listen, I am casting out demons and performing cures today and tomorrow, and on the third day I finish my work. Yet today, tomorrow, and the next day I must be on my way, because it is impossible for a prophet to be killed away from Jerusalem."

'Jerusalem, Jerusalem, the city that kills the prophets and stones those who are sent to it! How often have I desired to gather your children together as a hen gathers her brood under her wings, and you were not willing! See, your house is left to you. And I tell you, you will not see me until the time comes when you say, "Blessed is the one who comes in the name of the Lord." ' *Luke 13: 31-35*

A CANTICLE

SONG OF HUMILITY
Hosea 6: 1-6

1 Come, let us return to the Lord ▪
   who has torn us and will heal us.
2 God has stricken us ▪
   and will bind up our wounds.
3 After two days, he will revive us, ▪
   and on the third day will raise us up,
   that we may live in his presence.
4 Let us strive to know the Lord; ▪
   his appearing is as sure as the sunrise.
5 He will come to us like the showers, ▪
   like the spring rains that water the earth.
6 'O Ephraim, how shall I deal with you? ▪
   How shall I deal with you, O Judah?
7 'Your love for me is like the morning mist, ▪
   like the dew that goes early away.

Second Week of Lent

8 'Therefore, I have hewn them by the prophets, ▪
  and my judgement goes forth as the light.
9 'For loyalty is my desire and not sacrifice, ▪
  and the knowledge of God
       rather than burnt offerings.

Prayer

INTERCESSIONS AND THANKSGIVINGS

*Pray for those who contemptuously dismiss the claims of
    Christian faith,*
   *peace in Jerusalem between the three faiths with a
   common heritage from Abraham,*
   *for those whose faith has been damaged by bad
   experiences of the Church.*
Give thanks for committed peace-makers,
   *for those who visit and bring healing to those who are
   sick in body and mind,*
   *for all whose courage both encourages us
   and puts us to shame*

THE COLLECT LENT 2

Almighty God,
you show to those who are in error the light of your truth
that they may return to the way of righteousness:
Grant to all those who are admitted
into the fellowship of Christ's religion,
that they may reject those things
that are contrary to their profession,
and follow all such things
as are agreeable to the same;
through our Lord Jesus Christ. Amen.

or one of these prayers
O God of Abraham, Isaac and Jacob,
you called our ancestors to a journey of faith;
and in your Son, lifted up on the cross,
you opened for us the path to eternal life.
Grant that, being born again of water and the Spirit,
we may joyfully serve you in newness of life
and faithfully walk in your holy ways;
through Jesus Christ our Lord. Amen.

Uniting in Prayer II

God,
you have made known your love
through the life and words of Jesus.
Help us to receive his teaching,
to find the fulness of that love
and bring its fragrance to others.

Prayer Book of New Zealand

THE LORD'S PRAYER

AN ENDING

God, grant us to know what is right,
do what is just
and follow your purpose in all things;
through Christ our Lord. Amen.

Celebrating the Christian Year

The Third Week of Lent

Preparation

A SENTENCE OF SCRIPTURE

Our citizenship is in heaven, and it is from there that
we are expecting a Saviour, the Lord Jesus Christ.

Philippians 3: 20

A PRAYER OF PENITENCE

Almighty God,
look on us with mercy, we pray,
forgive us our sins, known and unknown,
things done and things left undone.
This we ask through the saving death of Jesus Christ,
in whose name alone is our hope. Amen.

HYMN

O love that wilt not let me go,
I rest my weary soul in thee:
I give thee back the life I owe,
that in thine ocean depths its flow
may richer, fuller be.

O light that followest all my way,
I yield my flickering torch to thee:
my heart restores its borrowed ray,
that in thy sunshine's blaze its day
may brighter, fairer be.

O joy that seekest me through pain,
I cannot close my heart to thee:
I trace the rainbow through the rain,
and feel the promise is not vain,
that morn shall tearless be.

O cross that liftest up my heard,
I dare not ask to fly from thee:
I lay in dust life's glory dead,
and from the ground there blossoms red
life that shall endless be.

George Matheson, 1842-1906

The Word of God

PSALM 63: 1-9

Lord, I love the house of your habitation ▪
and the place where your glory abides.

1 O God, you are my God; eagerly I seek you; ▪
   my soul is athirst for you.
2 My flesh also faints for you, ▪
   as in a dry and thirsty land where there is no water.
3 So would I gaze upon you in your holy place, ▪
   that I might behold your power and your glory.
4 Your loving-kindness is better than life itself ▪
   and so my lips shall praise you.
5 I will bless you as long as I live ▪
   and lift up my hands in your name.
6 My soul shall be satisfied,
      as with marrow and fatness, ▪
   and my mouth shall praise you with joyful lips,
7 When I remember you upon my bed ▪
   and meditate on you in the watches of the night.
8 For you have been my helper ▪
   and under the shadow of your wings will I rejoice.
9 My soul clings to you; ▪
   your right hand shall hold me fast.

A BIBLE READING

THE INWARD WORKING OF GOD

Monday	*Romans 2: 1-11*
Tuesday	*Romans 2: 12-16*
Wednesday	*Luke 13: 18-21*

GOD'S GRACIOUSNESS

Thursday	*2 Corinthians 4: 16-18*
Friday	*2 Corinthians 5: 16-21*
Saturday	*Luke 15: 3-10*

or

At that very time there were some present who told Jesus about the Galileans whose blood Pilate had mingled with their sacrifices. He asked them, 'Do you think that because these Galileans suffered in this way they were worse sinners than all other Galileans? No, I tell you; but unless you repent, you will all perish as they did. Or those eighteen who were killed when the tower of Siloam fell on them – do you think that they were worse offenders than all the others living in Jerusalem? No, I tell you; but unless you repent, you will all perish just as they did.'

Then he told this parable: 'A man had a fig tree planted in his vineyard; and he came looking for fruit on it and found none. So he said to the gardener, "See here! For three years I have come looking for fruit on this fig tree, and still I find none. Cut it down! Why should it be wasting the soil?" He replied, "Sir, let it alone for one more year, until I dig round it and put manure on it. If it bears fruit next year, well and good; but if not, you can cut it down."' *Luke 13: 1-9*

Third Week of Lent

URBS FORTITUDINIS
Isaiah 26: 1-4, 7, 8

1 We have a strong city ■
    salvation will God appoint for walls and bulwarks.
2 Open ye the gates ■
    that the righteous nation which keepeth the truth
        may enter in.
3 Thou wilt keep him in perfect peace
        whose mind is stayed on thee ■
    because he trusteth in thee.
4 Trust ye in the Lord for ever ■
    for our rock of ages is the Lord.
5 The way of the just is uprightness ■
    thou that art upright dost direct the path of the just.
6 Yea in the way of thy judgements O Lord
        have we waited for thee ■
    the desire of our soul is to thy Name
        and to the remembrance of thee.

Prayer

INTERCESSIONS AND THANKSGIVINGS

Pray for those struggling with addictions,
   for those who seek to bring stability to shaken lives,
   for those called to bring the good news of the Gospel to
   those on the fringe of society.
Give thanks for aid-workers
   especially those who bring healing and hope,
   for those who sacrificially give their lives
   to the 'service of the poor',
   for those who strive to bring wholeness to broken
   communities in places devastated
   through natural or human-caused disasters.

Third Week of Lent

THE COLLECT OF LENT 3

Merciful Lord,
Grant your people grace to withstand the temptations
of the world, the flesh and the devil
and with pure hearts and minds to follow you,
the only God;
through Jesus Christ our Lord. Amen.

or one of these prayers
Faithful God,
you desire that we turn away from things
    that do not satisfy
and find our fulfilment in you:
have patience with us,
tend and nurture our faith
that we may bear fruit
to the praise of your grace and majesty.
Grant this through Jesus Christ
who is one with you and the Holy Spirit,
    now and for ever. Amen.

Celebrating the Christian Year. altd

Lord, we look for you and long for you.
Our whole being thirsts for you and your love.
Open our eyes and awaken us to see you
    in your world, in other people
    and especially in those who suffer.
Shape us and transform us by your grace,
that we may grow in wisdom and in confidence,
never faltering until we have done all that you desire
to bring your kingdom of peace to fulfilment. Amen.

THE LORD'S PRAYER

AN ENDING

The Father keep us and protect us from all evil.
The Christ of the cross deliver us from darkness.
The Holy Spirit guide us in all goodness.

Third Week of Lent

The Fourth Week of Lent

Preparation

A SENTENCE OF SCRIPTURE

While the prodigal was still far off, his father saw him and was filled with compassion; he ran and put his arms around him and kissed him. *Luke 15: 20*

A PRAYER OF PENITENCE

Merciful and dependable Lord,
you reach out to us in mercy
even when we rebel and refuse to listen to your call.
We confess that we prefer to walk in disobedience
rather than in the way of your holy laws.
We seek your forgiveness
and pray that you will soften our hearts
 with the warmth of your saving love,
that we may know your Son alive within us,
redeeming us,
and raising us up into your eternal presence.
We pray in his name who was lifted up on the cross
to draw men and women everywhere to him. Amen.

RCL Prayers altd

HYMN

My song is love unknown,
my Saviour's love to me,
love to the loveless shown,
that they might lovely be.
O who am I,
that for my sake
my Lord should take
frail flesh and die?

He came from his blest throne,
salvation to bestow;
but men made strange, and none
the longed-for Christ would know.
But O, my friend,
my friend indeed,
who at my need
his life did spend.

Sometimes they strew his way,
and his sweet praises sing,
resounding all the day
Hosannas to their King.
Then 'Crucify!'
is all their breath,
and for his death
they thirst and cry.

Here might I stay and sing,
no story so divine;
never was love, dear King,
never was grief like thine!
This is my friend
in whose sweet praise
I all my days
could gladly spend.

Samuel Crossman, 1624-83

The Word of God

PSALM 32: 1-6

Make me a clean heart, O God ▪
and renew a right spirit within me.

1 Happy the one whose transgression is forgiven, ▪
   and whose sin is covered.

2 Happy the one to whom the Lord imputes no guilt, ▪
  and in whose spirit there is no guile.
3 For I held my tongue; ▪
  my bones wasted away through my groaning
    all the day long.
4 Your hand was heavy upon me day and night; ▪
  my moisture was dried up
    like the drought in summer.
5 Then I acknowledged my sin to you ▪
  and my iniquity I did not hide.
6 I said, 'I will confess my transgressions to the Lord,' ▪
  and you forgave the guilt of my sin.

A BIBLE READING

THE MESSIANIC BANQUET

Monday	*Revelation 19: 1-8*
Tuesday	*Revelation 19: 9-10*
Wednesday	*Luke 9: 10-17*

GOD AND HIS PEOPLE

Thursday	*Isaiah 43: 1-7*
Friday	*Isaiah 43: 8-15*
Saturday	*Exodus 12: 21-27*

or

Jesus told this parable: 'There was a man who had two sons. The younger of them said to his father, "Father, give me the share of the property that will belong to me." So he divided his property between them. A few days later the younger son gathered all he had and travelled to a distant country, and there he squandered his property in dissolute living. When he had spent everything, a severe famine took place throughout that country, and he began to be in need. So he went and hired himself out to one of the citizens of that country, who sent him to his fields to feed the pigs. He would gladly have filled himself with the pods that the pigs were eating; and no one gave him anything. But when he came to himself he said, "How many of my father's hired hands have bread enough and to spare, but here I am dying of hunger! I will get up and go to my father, and I will say to him, 'Father, I have sinned against heaven and before you; I am no longer worthy to be called your son; treat me like one of your hired hands.'" So he set off and went to his father. But while he was still far off, his father saw him and was filled with compassion; he ran and put his arms around him and kissed him. Then the son said to him, "Father, I have sinned against heaven and before you; I am no longer worthy to be called your son." But the father said to his slaves, "Quickly, bring out a robe – the best one – and put it on him; put a ring on his finger and sandals on his feet. And get the fatted calf and kill it, and let us eat and celebrate; for this son of mine was dead and is alive again; he was lost and is found!" And they began to celebrate.

'Now his elder son was in the field; and when he came and approached the house, he heard music and dancing. He called one of the slaves and asked what was going on. He replied, "Your brother has come, and your father has killed the fatted calf, because he has got him back safe and sound." Then he became angry and refused to go in. His father came out and began to plead with him. But he answered his father, "Listen! For all these years I have been working like a slave for you, and I have never disobeyed your command; yet you have never given me even a young goat so that I might celebrate with my friends. But when this son of yours came back, who has devoured your property with prostitutes, you killed the fatted calf for him!" Then the father said to him, "Son, you are always with me, and all that is mine is yours. But we had to celebrate and rejoice, because this brother of yours was dead and has come to life; he was lost and has been found."'

Luke 15: 11b-32

A CANTICLE

SONG OF THE WORD
Isaiah 55: 6-11

1. Seek the Lord while he may be found, ▪
   call upon him while he is near;
2. Let the wicked abandon their ways, ▪
   and the unrighteous their thoughts;
3. Return to the Lord, ▪
   who will have mercy;
   > to our God, who will richly pardon.
4. 'For my thoughts are not your thoughts, ▪
   neither are your ways my ways', says the Lord.
5. 'For as the heavens are higher than the earth, ▪
   so are my ways higher than your ways
   > and my thoughts than your thoughts.
6. 'As the rain and the snow come down from above, ▪
   and return not again but water the earth,
7. 'Bringing forth life and giving growth, ▪
   seed for sowing and bread to eat,
8. 'So is my word that goes forth from my mouth; ▪
   it will not return to me fruitless,
9. 'But it will accomplish that which I purpose, ▪
   and succeed in the task I gave it.'

Prayer

INTERCESSIONS AND THANKSGIVINGS

Pray for those who are searching for meaning in life,
  for those are called to proclaim the Gospel in a society
  that often sees no need to listen,
  for parents, especially single mothers, seeking to bring up
  their children in the fear and nurture of the Lord.
Give thanks for all opportunities to show love and
  compassion to others
  for those who are at this time seeking baptism or the gifts
  of the Holy Spirit in confirmation,
  for those whose Christian lives and witness have
  encouraged us in our discipleship

THE COLLECT OF LENT 4

Lord God
whose blessed Son our Saviour
gave his back to the smiters
and did not hide his face from shame:
Give us grace to endure the sufferings
  of this present time
with sure confidence in the glory that shall be revealed;
through Jesus Christ our Lord. Amen.

or one of these prayers
Gracious Father,
truly compassionate to all your children,
So fill us with your love,
that, rising above our weaknesses,
we may always remain true to Christ;
who lives and reigns with you and the Holy Spirit,
one God, for ever and ever. Amen.

Uniting in Prayer II altd.

Father of all mercy,
careless of your dignity
you look for us,
and welcome us home.
Give us the grace to love
as we have been loved;
in Jesus' name. Amen.

Uniting in Prayer II

THE LORD'S PRAYER

AN ENDING

As a mother comforts her children,
so the Lord comforts us.
Open our eyes to see and our hearts to rejoice,
and we shall flourish like golden fields of wheat.

Based on Isaiah 66: 13, 14

The Fifth Week of Lent

Preparation

A SENTENCE OF SCRIPTURE

One thing I do: forgetting what lies behind and straining forward to what lies ahead, I press on toward the goal for the prize of the upward call of God in Christ Jesus. *Philippians 3: 13-14*

A PRAYER OF PENITENCE

The gospel calls us to turn away from sin and be faithful to Christ. As we offer ourselves to him in penitence and faith, we renew our confidence and trust in his mercy.

Father, you raise the dead to life in the Spirit:
Lord, have mercy.

Lord Jesus, you bring pardon and peace to the sinner:
Christ, have mercy.

Comforter, you bring light to those in darkness:
Lord, have mercy.

HYMN

Let all mortal flesh keep silence
and with fear and trembling stand;
ponder nothing earthly-minded,
for with blessing in his hand
Christ our God to earth descendeth,
our full homage to demand.

King of kings, yet born of Mary,
as of old on earth he stood,
Lord of lords, in human vesture –
in the Body and the Blood –
he will give to all the faithful
his own self for heavenly food.

Rank on rank the host of heaven
spreads its vanguard on the way,
as the Light of light descendeth
from the realms of endless day,
that the powers of hell may vanish
as the darkness clears away.

At his feet the six-winged seraph,
cherubim with sleepless eye,
veil their faces to the presence,
as with ceaseless voice they cry,
Hallelujah, Hallelujah,
Hallelujah! Lord most High.

Greek Liturgy of Saint James, 6th century

The Word of God

PSALM 126

Though I walk through the valley of the shadow of death ▪
I will fear no evil.

1. When the Lord restored the fortunes of Zion, ▪
   then were we like those who dream.
2. Then was our mouth filled with laughter ▪
   and our tongue with songs of joy.
3. Then said they among the nations, ▪
   'The Lord has done great things for them.'
4. The Lord has indeed done great things for us, ▪
   and therefore we rejoiced.

5 Restore again our fortunes, O Lord, ▪
as the river beds of the desert.
6 Those who sow in tears ▪
shall reap with songs of joy.
7 Those who go out weeping, bearing the seed, ▪
will come back with shouts of joy,
> bearing their sheaves with them.

A BIBLE READING

GOD AND THE CROSS

Monday	*Hebrews 10: 19-25*
Tuesday	*1 John 2: 18-28*
Wednesday	*Luke 18: 31-34*

THE PASSION OF JESUS

Thursday	*Isaiah 53: 10-12*
Friday	*Hebrews 2: 10-18*
Saturday	*Luke 23: 1-13*

or

Six days before the Passover Jesus came to Bethany, the home of Lazarus, whom he had raised from the dead. There they gave a dinner for him. Martha served, and Lazarus was one of those at the table with him. Mary took a pound of costly perfume made of pure nard, anointed Jesus' feet, and wiped them with her hair. The house was filled with the fragrance of the perfume. But Judas Iscariot, one of his disciples (the one who was about to betray him), said, 'Why was this perfume not sold for three hundred denarii and the money given to the poor?' (He said this not because he cared about the poor, but because he was a thief; he kept the common purse and used to steal what was put into it.) Jesus said, 'Leave her alone. She bought it so that she

Fifth Week of Lent

might keep it for the day of my burial. You always have the poor with you, but you do not always have me.'

John 12: 1-8

A CANTICLE

SONG OF SOLOMON
Song of Songs 8: 6-7

1 Set me as a seal upon your heart, ▪
   as a seal upon your arm;
2 For love is strong as death,
      passion fierce as the grave; ▪
   its flashes are flashes of fire, a raging flame.
3 Many waters cannot quench love, ▪
   neither can the floods drown it.
4 If all the wealth of our house were offered for love, ▪
   it would be utterly scorned.

Prayer

INTERCESSIONS AND THANKSGIVINGS

Pray that the outreach of the Church at this season may
   bring many to faith in the one crucified to draw all
   people to him.

Pray for those who offer hospitality in Christ's name
   especially to the homeless and those who feel themselves
   to be unwanted.

Pray that for all who at the climax of this Passiontide will
   be baptized and brought into the family of the church.

Give thanks for faith, for the victory of the Passion
   and the hope which the Easter message brings.

THE COLLECT OF LENT 5

Most merciful God,
who by the death and resurrection
 of your Son Jesus Christ
delivered and saved the world:
Grant that by faith in him who suffered on the cross,
we may triumph in the power of his victory;
through Jesus Christ our Lord. Amen.

or one of these prayers
God of all generosity,
your grace is free, yet it demands our lives.
Help us to serve you, not counting the cost;
may we be poured out as a living sacrifice,
loving the world
for love of you
and the sake of Christ. Amen.

Uniting in Prayer II

Most generous God,
no human words or costly gifts
can ever express our thanks and praise
for all that you have done for us
 through Christ your Son.
Grant that we may gladly give you the one precious gift
that we have to bring,
the offering of our loyalty and love;
and enable us to walk in love for others,
as Christ loved us and gave himself up for us,
a fragrant offering and sacrifice to you.
We ask this through your Son, our Lord Jesus Christ.
Amen.
Uniting in Prayer II

Fifth Week of Lent

THE LORD'S PRAYER

AN ENDING

Saviour of the world,
by your cross and passion you have redeemed us,
save and help us, we humbly pray. Amen.

Holy Week : Monday, Tuesday and Wednesday

Preparation

A SENTENCE OF SCRIPTURE

Christ humbled himself and became obedient to the point of death – even death on a cross. Therefore God also highly exalted him and gave him the name that is above every name. *Philippians 2: 8-9*

A PRAYER OF PENITENCE

Merciful God,
we confess that we have sinned against you
in thought, word and deed,
by what we have done,
and by what we have left undone.
We have not loved you
with our whole heart, mind and strength;
we have not loved our neighbours as ourselves.
In your mercy forgive what we have been,
help us to amend what we are,
and direct what we shall be,
so that we may delight in your will
and walk in your ways,
to the glory of your holy name. Amen.

HYMN

Sweet the moments, rich in blessing,
which before the Cross I spend,
life and health and peace possessing,
from the sinners' dying Friend.

Here I find my hope of heaven,
while upon the Lamb I gaze;
loving much, and much forgiven,
let my heart o'erflow in praise.

For thy sorrows we adore thee,
for the pains that wrought our peace,
gracious Saviour, we implore thee,
in our souls thy love increase.

Lord, in ceaseless contemplation,
fix our hearts and eyes on thee,
till we raise thy full salvation,
and thine unveiled glory see.   *Walter Shirley, 1725-86*

The Word of God

PSALM 31: 1-5

Answer me, O Lord, for your love is kind ■
in your compassion, turn to me.

1 In you, O Lord, have I taken refuge;
    let me never be put to shame; ■
  deliver me in your righteousness.
2 Incline your ear to me; ■
  make haste to deliver me.
3 Be my strong rock, a fortress to save me,
    for you are my rock and my stronghold; ■
  guide me, and lead me for your name's sake.
4 Take me out of the net
    that they have laid secretly for me, ■
  for you are my strength.
5 Into your hands I commend my spirit, ■
  for you have redeemed me, O Lord God of truth.

A BIBLE READING

CHRIST CRUCIFIED

Monday	*Luke 19: 45 - 20: 8*
Tuesday	*Luke 20: 20-40*
Wednesday	*Luke 22: 1-13*

or

When day came, the assembly of the elders of the people, both chief priests and scribes, gathered together, and they brought Jesus to their council. They said, 'If you are the Messiah, tell us.' He replied, 'If I tell you, you will not believe; and if I question you, you will not answer. But from now on the Son of Man will be seated at the right hand of the power of God.' All of them asked, 'Are you, then, the Son of God?' He said to them, 'You say that I am.' Then they said, 'What further testimony do we need? We have heard it ourselves from his own lips!'

Then the assembly rose as a body and brought Jesus before Pilate. They began to accuse him, saying, 'We found this man perverting our nation, forbidding us to pay taxes to the emperor, and saying that he himself is the Messiah, a king.' Then Pilate asked him, 'Are you the king of the Jews?' He answered, 'You say so.' Then Pilate said to the chief priests and the crowds, 'I find no basis for an accusation against this man.' But they were insistent and said, 'He stirs up the people by teaching throughout all Judea, from Galilee where he began even to this place.'

When Pilate heard this, he asked whether the man was a Galilean. And when he learned that he was under Herod's jurisdiction, he sent him off to Herod, who was himself in Jerusalem at that time. When Herod saw Jesus, he was very glad, for he had been wanting to see him for a long time, because he had heard about him and was hoping to see him perform some sign. He questioned him at some length, but Jesus gave him no answer. The chief priests and the scribes stood by, vehemently accusing him. Even Herod with his soldiers treated him with contempt and mocked him; then he put an elegant robe on him, and sent him back to Pilate. That same day Herod and Pilate became friends with each other; before this they had been enemies.

Pilate then called together the chief priests, the leaders, and the people, and said to them, 'You brought me this man as one who was perverting the people; and here I have examined him in your presence and have not found this man guilty of any of your charges against him. Neither has Herod, for he sent him back to us. Indeed, he has done nothing to deserve death. I will therefore have him flogged and release him.'

Then they all shouted out together, 'Away with this fellow! Release Barabbas for us!' (This was a man who had been put in prison for an insurrection that had taken place in the city, and for murder.) Pilate, wanting to release Jesus, addressed them again; but they kept shouting, 'Crucify, crucify him!' A third time he said to them, 'Why, what evil has he done? I have found in him no ground for the sentence of death; I will therefore have him flogged and then release him.' But they kept urgently demanding with loud shouts that he should be crucified; and their voices prevailed. So Pilate gave his verdict that their demand should be granted. He released the man they asked for, the one who had been put in prison for insurrection and murder, and he handed Jesus over as they wished.   *Luke 22: 66 - 23: 25*

A SONG OF LAMENTATION
Lamentations 1: 12, 16a, b; 3: 19, 22-28, 31-33

1 Is it nothing to you, all you who pass by? ▪
 Look and see if there is any sorrow like my sorrow;
2 Which was brought upon me, ▪
 which the Lord inflicted
  on the day of his fierce anger.
3 For these things I weep;
  my eyes flow with tears; ▪
 for a comforter is far from me,
  one to revive my courage;
4 Remember my affliction and my bitterness, ▪
 the wormwood and the gall!
5 The steadfast love of the Lord never ceases, ▪
 his mercies never come to an end;
6 They are new every morning; ▪
 great is your faithfulness.
7 'The Lord is my portion', says my soul, ▪
 'therefore I will hope in him.'
8 The Lord is good to those who wait for him, ▪
 to the soul that seeks him.
9 It is good that we should wait quietly ▪
 for the salvation of the Lord.
10 It is good to bear the yoke in our youth; ▪
 to sit alone in silence when he has imposed it.
11 For the Lord will not reject for ever, ▪
 though he causes grief, he will have compassion,
12 According to the abundance of his steadfast love; ▪
 for he does not willingly afflict or grieve anyone.

Holy Week: Monday, Tuesday and Wednesday

Prayer

INTERCESSIONS AND THANKSGIVINGS

Pray for all God's hurting children in this weary world.
Pray for peace for all peoples in Christ Jesus.
Pray for the unity of all Christ's followers who draw near to
    the foot of the cross.
Give thanks for Christ' suffering and his victory.
Give thanks for new creation in Christ
    and all gifts of healing and forgiveness.

A COLLECT

Lord Jesus Christ,
you humbled yourself in taking the form of a servant
and in obedience died on the cross for our salvation:
give us the mind to follow you
and to proclaim you as Lord and King,
to the glory of God the Father. Amen.

or one of these prayers

Jesus, you come to reconcile, yet suffer violence;
help us to find the peace you offer,
and praise your name
even when other voices are raised against you;
for you are the servant king,
now and for ever. Amen.   *Uniting in Prayer II*

Eternal God,
in the cross of Jesus we see the cost of our sin
and the depth of your love:
In humble hope and fear
may we place at his feet
all that we have and all that we are,
through Jesus Christ our Lord. Amen.

Alternative Collects

THE LORD'S PRAYER

AN ENDING

Saviour of the world,
by your cross and passion you have redeemed us,
save and help us, we humbly pray. Amen.

Holy Week: Maundy Thursday, Good Friday, and Holy Saturday

Preparation

A SENTENCE OF SCRIPTURE

Here is my servant, whom I uphold,
my chosen, in whom I delight;
I have put my spirit upon him;
he will bring forth justice to the nations.   *Isaiah 42: 1*

A PRAYER OF PENITENCE

Lord God,
you sent your Son to reconcile us to yourself and to one another.
   Lord, have mercy.

Lord Jesus,
you heal the wounds of sin and division.
   Christ, have mercy.

Holy Spirit,
through you we put to death the sins of the body – and live.
   Lord, have mercy.

HYMN

O my Saviour, lifted
from the earth for me,
draw me, in thy mercy,
nearer unto thee.

Speed these lagging footsteps,
melt this heart of ice,
as I scan the marvels
of thy Sacrifice.

Lift my earth-bound longings,
fix them, Lord, above;
draw me with the magnet
of thy mighty love.

Lord, thine arms are stretching
ever far and wide,
to enfold thy children
to thy loving side.

And I come, O Jesus,
dare I turn away?
No, thy love hath conquered,
and I come today:

Bringing all my burdens,
sorrow, sin and care,
at thy feet I lay them,
and I leave them there. *W Walsham How, 1823-97*

The Word of God

PSALM 22: 1-11

Answer me, O Lord, for your love is kind ▪
in your compassion, turn to me.

1 My God, my God, why have you forsaken me, ▪
   and are so far from my salvation,
   from the words of my distress?
2 O my God, I cry in the daytime, but you do not answer; ▪
   and by night also, but I find no rest.
3 Yet you are the Holy One, ▪
   enthroned upon the praises of Israel.
4 Our forebears trusted in you; ▪
   they trusted, and you delivered them.

Maundy Thursday, Good Friday, Holy Saturday

5 They cried out to you and were delivered; ▪
  they put their trust in you and were not confounded.
6 But as for me, I am a worm and no man, ▪
  scorned by all and despised by the people.
7 All who see me laugh me to scorn; ▪
  they curl their lips and wag their heads, saying,
8 'He trusted in the Lord; let him deliver him; ▪
  let him deliver him, if he delights in him.'
9 But it is you that took me out of the womb ▪
  and laid me safe upon my mother's breast.
10 On you was I cast ever since I was born; ▪
  you are my God even from my mother's womb.
11 Be not far from me, for trouble is near at hand ▪
  and there is none to help.

A BIBLE READING

CHRIST CRUCIFIED

Thursday	*Luke 22: 14-23, 39-53*
Friday	*Luke 23: 1- 49*
Saturday	*Luke 23: 50-56*

or

Two others also, who were criminals, were led away to be put to death with him. When they came to the place that is called The Skull, they crucified Jesus there with the criminals, one on his right and one on his left. Then Jesus said, 'Father, forgive them; for they do not know what they are doing.' And they cast lots to divide his clothing. And the people stood by, watching; but the leaders scoffed at him, saying, 'He saved others; let him save himself if he is the Messiah of God, his chosen one!' The soldiers also mocked him, coming up and offering him sour wine, and saying, 'If you are the King of the Jews, save yourself!' There was also an inscription over him,

'This is the King of the Jews.'

One of the criminals who were hanged there kept deriding him and saying, 'Are you not the Messiah? Save yourself and us!' But the other rebuked him, saying, 'Do you not fear God, since you are under the same sentence of condemnation? And we indeed have been condemned justly, for we are getting what we deserve for our deeds, but this man has done nothing wrong.' Then he said, 'Jesus, remember me when you come into your kingdom.' Jesus replied, 'Truly I tell you, today you will be with me in Paradise.'

It was now about noon, and darkness came over the whole land until three in the afternoon, while the sun's light failed; and the curtain of the temple was torn in two. Then Jesus, crying with a loud voice, said, 'Father, into your hands I commend my spirit.' Having said this, he breathed his last. When the centurion saw what had taken place, he praised God and said, 'Certainly this man was innocent.' And when all the crowds who had gathered there for this spectacle saw what had taken place, they returned home, beating their breasts. But all his acquaintances, including the women who had followed him from Galilee, stood at a distance, watching these things.

Luke 23: 32-49

A CANTICLE

A SONG OF LAMENTATION
Lamentations 1: 12, 16a, b; 3: 19, 22-28, 31-33

1 Is it nothing to you, all you who pass by? ▪
   Look and see if there is any sorrow like my sorrow;
2 Which was brought upon me, ▪
   which the Lord inflicted
      on the day of his fierce anger.
3 For these things I weep;
      my eyes flow with tears; ▪
   for a comforter is far from me,
      one to revive my courage;
4 Remember my affliction and my bitterness, ▪
   the wormwood and the gall!
5 The steadfast love of the Lord never ceases, ▪
   his mercies never come to an end;
6 They are new every morning; ▪
   great is your faithfulness.
7 'The Lord is my portion', says my soul, ▪
   'therefore I will hope in him.'
8 The Lord is good to those who wait for him, ▪
   to the soul that seeks him.
9 It is good that we should wait quietly ▪
   for the salvation of the Lord.
10 It is good to bear the yoke in our youth; ▪
   to sit alone in silence when he has imposed it.
11 For the Lord will not reject for ever, ▪
   though he causes grief, he will have compassion,
12 According to the abundance of his steadfast love; ▪
   for he does not willingly afflict or grieve anyone.

Prayer

INTERCESSIONS AND THANKSGIVINGS

Pray for all God's hurting children in this weary world,
for peace for all peoples in Christ Jesus,
for the unity of all Christ's followers who draw near to
the foot of the cross.
Give thanks for Christ's suffering and his victory,
for new creation in Christ and all gifts of healing and
forgiveness.

A COLLECT

O God,
who by the passion of your blessed Son made
an instrument of shameful death
to be for us the means of life:
Grant us so to glory in the cross of Christ,
that we may gladly suffer pain and loss
for the sake of your Son our Saviour Jesus Christ;
who lives and reigns with you and the Holy Spirit,
one God, now and for ever. Amen.

Collect of the Wednesday in Holy Week

or one of these prayers
Thirsting on the cross,
your Son shared the reproach of the oppressed
and carried the sins of all;
in him, O God, may the despairing find you,
the afflicted gain life
and the whole creation know its true king,
Jesus Christ our Lord. Amen

Michael Vasey, 1946-98

Eternal God,
in the cross of Jesus we see the cost of our sin
and the depth of your love:
In humble hope and fear
may we place at his feet
all that we have and all that we are,
through Jesus Christ our Lord. Amen.

Alternative Collects

THE LORD'S PRAYER

AN ENDING

Saviour of the world,
by your cross and passion you have redeemed us,
save and help us, we humbly pray. Amen.

The First Week of Easter

Preparation

A SENTENCE OF SCRIPTURE

Christ has been raised from the dead, the first fruits of those who have died. For as all die in Adam, so all will be made alive in Christ. *1 Corinthians 15: 20, 22*

A PRAYER OF PENITENCE

Almighty God,
in raising Jesus from the tomb,
you destroyed the power of death.
Hear us as we confess our failure to live
   by the good news of the resurrection.
Grant us the radiant power of your grace:
forgive, heal and renew us,
so that we may know and share the joy of life abundant,
given in Jesus Christ, our risen Lord.

Lutheran Renewal Worship altd.

HYMN

Jesus lives! thy terrors now
can no more, O death, appal us;
Jesus lives! by this we know
thou, O grave, canst not enthral us.
Hallelujah!

Jesus lives! henceforth is death
but the gate of life immortal:
this shall calm our trembling breath,
when we pass its gloomy portal.
Hallelujah!

Jesus lives! for us he died;
then, alone to Jesus living,
pure in heart may we abide,
glory to our Saviour giving.
Hallelujah!

Jesus lives! our hearts know well
naught from us his love shall sever;
life nor death nor powers of hell
tear us from his keeping ever.
Hallelujah!

Jesus lives! to him the throne
over all the world is given:
may we go where he is gone,
rest and reign with him in heaven.
Hallelujah!   *Christian F. Gellert, 1515-69*

The Word of God

PSALM 118: 1, 2, 14, 19-24

The Lord is risen from the tomb ▪
Alleluia.

1 O give thanks to the Lord, for he is good; ▪
   his mercy endures for ever.
2 Let Israel now proclaim, ▪
   'His mercy endures for ever.'
14 The Lord is my strength and my song, ▪
   and he has become my salvation.
19 Open to me the gates of righteousness, ▪
   that I may enter and give thanks to the Lord.
20 This is the gate of the Lord; ▪
   the righteous shall enter through it.
21 I will give thanks to you, for you have answered me ▪
   and have become my salvation.

22 The stone which the builders rejected ▪
 has become the chief cornerstone.
23 This is the Lord's doing, ▪
 and it is marvellous in our eyes.
24 This is the day that the Lord has made; ▪
 we will rejoice and be glad in it.

A BIBLE READING

CHRIST THE LORD IS RISEN

Monday	*1 Corinthians 5: 6b-8*
Tuesday	*Luke 24: 13-35*
Wednesday	*Luke 24: 36-44*
Thursday	*Luke 24: 45-49*
Friday	*Acts 5: 12-16*
Saturday	*Acts 5: 17-32*

(These selections are not from RCL Daily Readings)

or

On the first day of the week, at early dawn, the women came to the tomb, taking the spices that they had prepared. They found the stone rolled away from the tomb, but when they went in, they did not find the body. While they were perplexed about this, suddenly two men in dazzling clothes stood beside them. The women were terrified and bowed their faces to the ground, but the men said to them, 'Why do you look for the living among the dead? He is not here, but has risen. Remember how he told you, while he was still in Galilee, that the Son of Man must be handed over to sinners, and be crucified, and on the third day rise

Second Week of Easter

again.' Then they remembered his words, and returning from the tomb, they told all this to the eleven and to all the rest. Now it was Mary Magdalene, Joanna, Mary the mother of James, and the other women with them who told this to the apostles. But these words seemed to them an idle tale, and they did not believe them. But Peter got up and ran to the tomb; stooping and looking in, he saw the linen cloths by themselves; then he went home, amazed at what had happened.

Luke 24: 1-12

A CANTICLE

THE EASTER ANTHEMS
1 Corinthians 5: 7, 8 Romans 6: 9-11, 1 Cor 15: 20-22

1 Christ our passover has been sacrificed for us ▪
   therefore let us celebrate the feast.
2 Not with the old leaven of corruption
      and wickedness ▪
   but with the unleavened bread of sincerity and truth.
3 Christ once raised from the dead dies no more ▪
   death has no more dominion over him.
4 In dying he died to sin once for all ▪
   in living he lives to God.
5 See yourselves therefore as dead to sin ▪
   and alive to God in Jesus Christ our Lord.
6 Christ has been raised from the dead ▪
   the firstfruits of those who sleep.
7 For as by man came death ▪
   by man has come also the resurrection of the dead.
8 For as in Adam all die ▪
   even so in Christ shall all be made alive.

Prayer

INTERCESSIONS AND THANKSGIVINGS

Pray for the Church worldwide,
   the community of the resurrection,
   for courageous witness and bold proclamation,
   for all who are in pain or grieving over loved ones
   who have died, that they may know
   the comfort of God's love
   and the assurance of Easter hope.
Rejoice in Christ's Victory over sin, evil and death.
Give thanks for our foretaste of eternal life
   in baptism and eucharist.

THE COLLECT OF EASTER

Almighty God,
through your only-begotten Son Jesus Christ
you have overcome death
and opened to us the gate of everlasting life:
Grant that, as by your grace going before us
you put into our minds good desires,
so by your continual help
   we may bring them to good effect;
through Jesus Christ our Risen Lord
who is alive and reigns with you and the Holy Spirit,
one God, now and for ever. Amen.

or one of these prayers
Living God,
for our redemption you gave your only-begotten Son
to the death of the cross,
and by his glorious resurrection
have delivered us from the power of our enemy:
grant us so to die daily unto sin,

First Week of Easter

that we may evermore live with him
    in the joy of his risen life;
through Jesus Christ our Lord. Amen.

Post Communion Prayer

Give to us, Lord, that gift greater than grace:
your presence and your very self,
broken for our salvation,
raised to bring us life
in Jesus Christ our Lord;
in whose name we ask.   *Common Worship Daily Prayer*

THE LORD'S PRAYER

AN ENDING

May the love of the Cross,
the power of the Resurrection,
and the presence of living Lord
be with us always. Amen.

The Second Week of Easter

Preparation

A SENTENCE OF SCRIPTURE

Peter said: The God of our ancestors raised Jesus from the dead ... [and] exalted him to his own right hand as Prince and Saviour. *Acts 5: 30, 31 TNIV*

A PRAYER OF PENITENCE

Lord God, you raised your Son from the dead.
Lord, have mercy.

Lord Jesus, through you we are more than conquerors.
Christ, have mercy.

Holy Spirit, you help us in our weakness.
Lord, have mercy.

HYMN

Hark, ten thousand voices sounding
far and wide throughout the sky,
'tis the voice of joy abounding,
Jesus lives, no more to die.

Jesus lives, his conflict over,
lives to claim his great reward;
angels round the Victor hover,
crowding to behold their Lord.

Yonder throne for him erected
now becomes the Victor's seat;
lo, the Man on earth rejected
angels worship at his feet.

All the powers of heaven adore him,
all obey his sovereign word;
day and night they cry before him,
'Holy, Holy, Holy, Lord!' *Thomas Kelly, 1769-1854*

The Word of God

PSALM 150

The Lord has been mindful of us and he will bless us. ▪
Alleluia.

1. Alleluia.
   O praise God in his holiness; ▪
   praise him in the firmament of his power.
2. Praise him for his mighty acts; ▪
   praise him according to his excellent greatness.
3. Praise him with the blast of the trumpet; ▪
   praise him upon the harp and lyre.
4. Praise him with timbrel and dances; ▪
   praise him upon the strings and pipe.
5. Praise him with ringing cymbals; ▪
   praise him upon the clashing cymbals.
6. Let everything that has breath ▪
   praise the Lord.
   Alleluia.

A BIBLE READING

CONFESSING THE RISEN LORD

Monday	*Revelation 1: 9-20*
Tuesday	*Revelation 2: 8-11*
Wednesday	*Luke 12: 4-12*
Thursday	*Revelation 3: 14-22*
Friday	*Revelation 4: 1-11*
Saturday	*Luke 14: 12-14*

or

When the temple police had brought the apostles, they had them stand before the council. The high priest questioned them, saying, 'We gave you strict orders not to teach in this name, yet here you have filled Jerusalem with your teaching and you are determined to bring this man's blood on us.' But Peter and the apostles answered, 'We must obey God rather than any human authority. The God of our ancestors raised up Jesus, whom you had killed by hanging him on a tree. God exalted him at his right hand as Leader and Saviour, so that he might give repentance to Israel and forgiveness of sins. And we are witnesses to these things, and so is the Holy Spirit whom God has given to those who obey him.' *Acts of the Apostles 5: 27-32*

A CANTICLE

A SONG OF FAITH
Based on 1 Peter 1: 3-4, 18-21

1 Blessed be the God and Father ▪
  of our Lord Jesus Christ!
2 By his great mercy we have been born anew
   to a living hope ▪
  through the resurrection of Jesus Christ
   from the dead.
3 Into an inheritance that is imperishable,
   undefiled and unfading, ▪
  kept in heaven for us.
4 Who are being protected by the power of God ▪
  through faith for a salvation,
   ready to be revealed in the last time.
5 Ransomed from the futile ways of your ancestors ▪

    not with perishable things like silver or gold
6 But with the precious blood of Christ ■
    like that of a lamb without spot or stain.
7 Through him we have confidence in God, ■
    who raised him from the dead and gave him glory,
        so that our faith and hope are set on God.

Prayer

INTERCESSIONS AND THANKSGIVINGS

Pray for all those who have been ordained
*   and sent as ministers of reconciliation*
*   and for all preparing for ordination.*
Pray for those witnessing for Christ in inhospitable
*   circumstances or in lands where society is hostile to the*
*   Christian message*
Give thanks for the those who boldly witness to the power of
*   the resurrection by lives dedicated to the service of others.*
Give thanks for all who have encouraged us
*   in our pilgrimage in faith .*

THE COLLECT OF EASTER 2

Almighty Father,
you have given your only Son to die for our sins
and to rise again for our justification:
Grant us so to put away the leaven
of malice and wickedness
that we may always serve you
   in pureness of living and truth;
through the merits of your Son Jesus Christ our Lord.

Amen

or one of these prayers

You come into our midst, Lord Jesus;
you hold out your scarred hands,
and surprise us with hope.
Help us to receive your word and your Spirit,
that in our woundedness
we may know you as our life,
now and for ever. Amen.

Uniting in Prayer II

Risen Christ,
for whom no door is locked, no entrance barred:
open the doors of our hearts,
that we may seek the good of others
and walk the joyful road of sacrifice and peace,
to the praise of God the Father. Amen.

Alternative Collects

THE LORD'S PRAYER

AN ENDING

The God of peace, who brought again from the dead our Lord Jesus, the great shepherd of the sheep, by the blood of the eternal covenant, make us perfect in everything good to do his will, working among us that which is well-pleasing in his sight, through Jesus Christ, to whom be glory for ever and ever. *Hebrews 13; 20, 21*

The Third Week of Easter

Preparation

A SENTENCE OF SCRIPTURE

Worthy is the Lamb who was slain, to receive power and wealth, wisdom and might, honour and glory and praise! *Revelation 5: 12*

A PRAYER OF PENITENCE

God of all mercy;
we confess that we have sinned against you.
We have failed to honour you
in what we have done, in what we have said
   and in what we have thought.
We have failed to honour you in other people.
Forgive, restore and strengthen us
through our risen Lord Jesus Christ,
that we may dwell in your love
and serve only your will
for your people and for your creation. Amen.

HYMN

Awake and sing the song
of Moses and the Lamb;
wake every heart and every tongue
to praise the Saviour's Name.

Sing of his dying love,
sing of his rising power,
sing how he intercedes above
for those whose sins he bore.

Sing on your heavenly way,
ye ransomed sinners, sing;
sing on, rejoicing every day
in Christ the eternal King!

Soon shall ye hear him say,
'Ye blessed children, come';
soon will he call us hence away
and take his wanderers home.

There shall each heart and tongue
his endless praise proclaim,
and sweeter voices swell the song
of Moses and the Lamb. *William Hammond, 1719-83*

The Word of God

PSALM 30

The Lord is my light and my salvation. ▪
Whom then shall I fear?

1 I will exalt you, O Lord,
    because you have raised me up ▪
  and have not let my foes triumph over me.
2 O Lord my God, I cried out to you ▪
  and you have healed me.
3 You brought me up, O Lord, from the dead; ▪
  you restored me to life
    from among those that go down to the Pit.
4 Sing to the Lord, you servants of his; ▪
  give thanks to his holy name.
5 For his wrath endures but the twinkling of an eye,
    his favour for a lifetime. ▪
  Heaviness may endure for a night,
    but joy comes in the morning.

6 In my prosperity I said, 'I shall never be moved. ∎
You, Lord, of your goodness,
  have made my hill so strong.'
7 Then you hid your face from me ∎
and I was utterly dismayed.
8 To you, O Lord, I cried; ∎
to the Lord I made my supplication:
9 'What profit is there in my blood,
  if I go down to the Pit? ∎
Will the dust praise you or declare your faithfulness?
10 'Hear, O Lord, and have mercy upon me; ∎
O Lord, be my helper.'
11 You have turned my mourning into dancing; ∎
you have put off my sackcloth
  and girded me with gladness;
12 Therefore my heart sings to you without ceasing; ∎
O Lord my God, I will give you thanks for ever.

A BIBLE READING

CHANGED LIVES

Monday	*Acts 9: 19b-31*
Tuesday	*Acts 26:1-8*
Wednesday	*Luke 5: 1-11*

THE GOOD SHEPHERD

Thursday	*Ezekiel 11: 1-25*
Friday	*Ezekiel 28: 25-26*
Saturday	*Luke 12: 29-32*

or

Jesus showed himself again to the disciples by the Sea of Tiberias; and he showed himself in this way. Gathered there together were Simon Peter, Thomas called the Twin, Nathanael of Cana in Galilee, the sons of Zebedee, and two others of his disciples. Simon Peter said to them, 'I am going fishing.' They said to him, 'We will go with you.' They went out and got into the boat, but that night they caught nothing.

Just after daybreak, Jesus stood on the beach; but the disciples did not know that it was Jesus. Jesus said to them, 'Children, you have no fish, have you?' They answered him, 'No.' He said to them, 'Cast the net to the right side of the boat, and you will find some.' So they cast it, and now they were not able to haul it in because there were so many fish. That disciple whom Jesus loved said to Peter, 'It is the Lord!' When Simon Peter heard that it was the Lord, he put on some clothes, for he was naked, and jumped into the lake. But the other disciples came in the boat, dragging the net full of fish, for they were not far from the land, only about a hundred yards off.

When they had gone ashore, they saw a charcoal fire there, with fish on it, and bread. Jesus said to them, 'Bring some of the fish that you have just caught.' So Simon Peter went aboard and hauled the net ashore, full of large fish, a hundred and fifty-three of them; and though there were so many, the net was not torn. Jesus said to them, 'Come and have breakfast.' Now none of the disciples dared to ask him, 'Who are you?' because they knew it was the Lord. Jesus came and took the bread and gave it to them, and did the same with the fish. This was now the third time that Jesus appeared to the disciples after he was raised from the dead.

When they had finished breakfast, Jesus said to Simon Peter, 'Simon son of John, do you love me more than these?' He said to him, 'Yes, Lord; you know that I love you.' Jesus said to him, 'Feed my lambs.' A second time he said to him, 'Simon son of John, do you love me?' He said to him, 'Yes, Lord; you know that I love you.' Jesus said to him, 'Tend my sheep.' He said to him the third time, 'Simon son of John, do you love me?' Peter felt hurt because he said to him the third time, 'Do you love me?' And he said to him, 'Lord, you know everything; you know that I love you.' Jesus said to him, 'Feed my sheep. Very truly, I tell you, when you were younger, you used to fasten your own belt and go wherever you wished. But when you grow old, you will stretch out your hands, and someone else will fasten a belt around you and take you where you do not wish to go.' He said this to indicate the kind of death by which he would glorify God. After this he said to him, 'Follow me.' *John 21: 1-19*

A CANTICLE

GLORY AND HONOUR
Revelation 4: 11 and 5:9, 10, 13b

1 Glory and honour and power ▪
   are yours by right O Lord our God.
2 For your created all things ▪
   and by your will they have their being.
3 Glory and honour and power ▪
   are yours by right O Lamb for us slain;
4 For by your blood you ransomed us for God ▪
   from every race and language
      from every people and nation.
5 To make us a kingdom of priests ▪
   to stand and serve before our God.
6 To him who sits on the throne and to the Lamb ▪
   be praise and honour glory and might
   for ever and ever. Amen.

Prayer

INTERCESSIONS AND THANKSGIVINGS

Pray for those called to leadership in your Church, that they
   may be entirely centred on obeying Christ.
Pray that in worship congregations may more clearly
   demonstrate that the Resurrection of Jesus has changed
   their lives.
Give thanks for being able to worship freely
   and for access to the Holy Scriptures.
Give thanks for all relationships
   in which we have known caring love.

THE COLLECT OF EASTER 3

Almighty Father,
who in your great mercy gladdened the disciples
with the sight of the risen Lord:
Give us such knowledge of his presence with us,
that we may be strengthened
and sustained by his risen life
and serve you continually in righteousness and truth;
through Jesus Christ our Lord. Amen.

or one of these prayers
Living God,
Christ is indeed worthy of all praise;
he died, and is risen from the dead.
Feed us with your grace,
that in times of success or failure
we may find life in following you
for the sake of Jesus the Lord. Amen.

Uniting in Prayer II

God of heaven and earth:
you are glorified in the different gifts
 you give to each disciple.
Let your praises in heaven be echoed on earth
in the worship and ministry of your people,
so that your Church may flourish in diversity
and be strong in the unity which the Spirit gives;
through Jesus Christ our Lord. Amen.

THE LORD'S PRAYER

AN ENDING

Praise to you, Lord Jesus.
Dying, you destroyed our death,
rising you restored our life.
Lord Jesus, come in glory.

The Fourth Week of Easter

Preparation

A SENTENCE OF SCRIPTURE

Jesus said: My sheep hear my voice. I know them, and they follow me; I give them eternal life.   *John 10: 27-28*

A PRAYER OF PENITENCE

Heavenly Father,
we have sinned against you and against our neighbour
in thought and word and deed,
through negligence, through weakness,
through our own deliberate fault;
by what we have done
and by what we have failed to do.
We are truly sorry and repent of all our sins.
For the sake of your Son Jesus Christ who died for us,
forgive us all that is past;
and grant that we may serve you in newness of life
to the glory of your name. Amen.

HYMN

Ye choirs of new Jerusalem,
your sweetest notes employ,
your Paschal victory to hymn
in strains of holy joy.

For Judah's lion bursts his chains,
crushing the serpent's head,
and cries aloud through death's domains
to wake the imprisoned dead.

Devouring depths of hell their prey
at his command restore;
his ransomed hosts pursue their way
where Jesus goes before.

Triumphant in his glory now,
to him all power is given;
to him in one communion bow
all saints in earth and heaven.

While we, his soldiers, praise our King,
his mercy we implore,
within his palace bright to bring
and keep us evermore.

All glory to the Father be,
all glory to the Son,
all glory, Holy Ghost, to thee,
while endless ages run. *Saint Fulbert, died 1028*

The Word of God

PSALM 23

The Lord is our God ▪
we are the people of his pasture and the sheep of his hand.

1 The Lord is my shepherd; ▪
 therefore can I lack nothing.
2 He makes me lie down in green pastures ▪
 and leads me beside still waters.
3 He will refresh my soul ▪
 and guide me in the paths of righteousness
  for his name's sake.
4 Though I walk through the valley of the shadow of
  death, I shall fear no evil; ▪
 for you are with me; your rod and your staff,
  they comfort me.

5 You spread a table before me
   in the presence of those who trouble me; ▪
   you have anointed my head with oil
      and my cup will be full.
6 Surely goodness and loving mercy will follow me
      all the days of my life, ▪
   and I shall dwell in the house of the Lord for ever.

A BIBLE READING

UNITING AND HEALING

Monday	*Ezekiel 37: 15-28*
Tuesday	*Acts 9: 32-35*
Wednesday	*John 10: 31-42*

VISIONS OF GOD'S REIGN

Thursday	*Revelation 10: 1-11*
Friday	*Revelation 11: 15-19*
Saturday	*Matthew 24: 36-44*

or

The festival of the Dedication took place in Jerusalem. It was winter, and Jesus was walking in the temple, in the portico of Solomon. So the Jews gathered around him and said to him, 'How long will you keep us in suspense? If you are the Messiah, tell us plainly.' Jesus answered, 'I have told you, and you do not believe. The works that I do in my Father's name testify to me; but you do not believe, because you are not my sheep. My sheep hear my voice. I know them, and they follow me. I give them eternal life, and they will never perish. No one will snatch them out of my hand. What my Father has given me is greater than all else, and no one can snatch it out of the Father's hand. The Father and I are one.'
John 10: 22-30

THE SONG OF ISAIAH
Isaiah 12: 2-6

1 Surely God is my salvation; ▪
   I will trust, and will not be afraid:
2 for the Lord God is my strength and my might; ▪
   he has become my salvation.
3 With joy you will draw water
      from the wells of salvation ▪
   And you will say in that day:
      Give thanks to the Lord, call on his name;
4 Make known his deeds among the nations: ▪
   proclaim that his name is exalted.
5 Sing praises to the Lord, for he has done gloriously ▪
   let this be known in all the earth.
6 Shout aloud and sing for joy, O royal Zion, ▪
   for great in your midst is the Holy One of Israel.

Prayer

INTERCESSIONS AND THANKSGIVINGS

Pray for greater urgency in the search for unity in the worldwide church of Jesus Christ for becoming one flock with one Lord.

Pray that all called to pastor the flock of Christ in the dangers of the world today, especially in places where professing Christian faith lays a person in great personal danger.

Give thanks for the difference knowing Christ makes to life itself.

Give thanks for all who venture into dangerous places in the service of humanity and the lost sheep of Christ's flock.

THE COLLECT OF EASTER 4

Almighty God,
whose Son Jesus Christ is the resurrection and the life:
Raise us, who trust in him,
from the death of sin to the life of righteousness,
that we may seek those things which are above,
where he reigns with you and the Holy Spirit,
one God, now and for ever. Amen.

or one of these prayers
Risen Christ,
faithful shepherd of your Father's sheep:
teach us to hear your voice
and to follow your command,
that all your people may be gathered into one flock,
to the glory of God the Father. Amen.

Alternative Collects

O Jesus,
you are the Shepherd
you call us by name;
you are the Lamb
you gave yourself for our sakes.
May we rest in the palm of your hand,
and find the salvation you freely give;
this we ask in your name. Amen.

Uniting in Prayer II altd.

Fourth Week of Easter

THE LORD'S PRAYER

AN ENDING

Lord Jesus,
make us a people
whose song is alleluia,
whose sign is peace
and whose name is love,
and you are all in all.

The Fifth Week of Easter

Preparation

A SENTENCE OF SCRIPTURE

By this everyone will know that you are my disciples, if you have love for one another. *John 13: 35*

A PRAYER OF PENITENCE

Almighty God, our heavenly Father,
we have sinned in thought and word and deed,
and in what we have left undone.
We are truly sorry and we humbly repent.
For the sake of your Son, Jesus Christ,
have mercy on us and forgive us,
that we may walk in newness of life
to the glory of your name. Amen.

HYMN

Hail, thou once despised Jesus!
hail, thou Galilean King!
Thou didst suffer to release us,
thou didst free salvation bring:
hail, thou universal Saviour,
bearer of our sin and shame;
by thy merits we find favour;
life is given through thy Name.

Paschal Lamb! by God appointed,
all our sins on thee were laid;
by almighty love anointed,
thou hast full atonement made:
all thy people are forgiven
through the virtue of thy Blood,
opened is the gate of heaven,
peace is made 'twixt man and God.

Jesus, hail! enthroned in glory,
there for ever to abide;
all the heavenly hosts adore thee,
seated at thy Father's side:
there for sinners thou art pleading,
there thou dost our place prepare,
ever for us interceding,
till in glory we appear.   *John Bakewell, 1721-1819*

The Word of God

PSALM 148: 7-14

Praise the Lord, O my soul ▪
while I live will I praise the Lord.

7 Praise the Lord from the earth, ▪
   you sea monsters and all deeps;
8 Fire and hail, snow and mist, ▪
   tempestuous wind, fulfilling his word;
9 Mountains and all hills, ▪
   fruit trees and all cedars;
10 Wild beasts and all cattle, ▪
   creeping things and birds on the wing;
11 Kings of the earth and all peoples, ▪
   princes and all rulers of the world;
12 Young men and women, old and young together; ▪
   let them praise the name of the Lord.

13 For his name only is exalted, ▪
   his splendour above earth and heaven.
14 He has raised up the horn of his people
      and praise for all his faithful servants, ▪
   the children of Israel, a people who are near him.
   Alleluia.

A BIBLE READING

LOVE YOUR NEIGHBOUR

Monday	*Acts 11: 19-26*
Tuesday	*Acts 11: 27-30*
Wednesday	*Luke 10: 25-28*

GOD'S WISDOM

Thursday	*Proverbs 2: 1-5*
Friday	*Proverbs 2: 6-8*
Saturday	*Luke 19: 1-10*

or

During supper, when Judas had gone out, Jesus said, 'Now the Son of Man has been glorified, and God has been glorified in him. If God has been glorified in him, God will also glorify him in himself and will glorify him at once. Little children, I am with you only a little longer. You will look for me; and as I said to the Jews so now I say to you, "Where I am going, you cannot come." I give you a new commandment, that you love one another. Just as I have loved you, you also should love one another. By this everyone will know that you are my disciples, if you have love for one another.'

John 13: 31-35

Fifth Week of Easter

A CANTICLE

BLESS THE LORD

The Song of the Three 29-34

1 Bless the Lord the God of our fathers ▪
 sing his praise and exalt him for ever.
2 Bless his holy and glorious name ▪
 sing his praise and exalt him for ever.
3 Bless him in his holy and glorious temple ▪
 sing his praise and exalt him for ever.
4 Bless him who beholds the depths ▪
 sing his praise and exalt him for ever.
5 Bless him seated between the cherubim ▪
 sing his praise and exalt him for ever.
6 Bless him on the throne of his kingdom ▪
 sing his praise and exalt him for ever.
7 Bless him in the heights of heaven ▪
 sing his praise and exalt him for ever.
8 Bless the Father the Son and the Holy Spirit ▪
 sing his praise and exalt him for ever.

Prayer

INTERCESSIONS AND THANKSGIVINGS

Pray that the members of the Church may show such caring love for one another that others will be drawn to Christ.

Pray for all who mourn, for those are seriously ill and for all who have lost hope; that in Jesus they may find peace and comfort.

Give thanks for writers whose books have helped men and women to find faith.

Give thanks for all who minister to those who have lost loved ones, especially in tragic circumstances.

THE COLLECT OF EASTER 5

Lord of all life and power,
who through the mighty resurrection of your Son
overcame the old order of sin and death
to make all things new in him:
Grant that we, being dead to sin
and alive to you in Jesus Christ,
may reign with him in glory;
to whom with you and the Holy Spirit
be praise and honour, glory and might,
now and in all eternity. Amen.

or one of these prayers
Almighty Father,
whose Son, our Lord Jesus Christ,
is the light of the world:
set us on fire with the Spirit of power,
that, in everything we think and say and do,
we may proclaim the wonder of Christ's resurrection.
He lives and reigns with you and the Holy Spirit,
one God, for ever and ever. Amen.

Uniting in Prayer II

Risen Christ,
your wounds declare your love for the world
and the wonder of your risen life:
Give us compassion and courage
to risk ourselves for those we serve,
to the glory of God the Father. Amen.

Alternative Collects

THE LORD'S PRAYER

AN ENDING

May your salvation, Lord,
be always ours,
this day and evermore. Amen.

The Sixth Week of Easter

Preparation

A SENTENCE OF SCRIPTURE

Jesus said: Anyone who loves me will obey my teaching. My Father will love them, and we will come to them and make our home with them.

John 14: 23 TNIV

A PRAYER OF PENITENCE

Father, we confess to you
our lack of care for the world you have given us.
Lord, have mercy.

Lord Jesus, we confess to you
our selfishness in not sharing our good things
with your brothers and sisters in need.
Christ, have mercy.

Holy Spirit, we confess to you
our failure to respond to your prompting
to protect resources for others.
Lord, have mercy.

HYMN

Fill thou my life, O Lord my God,
in every part with praise,
that my whole being may proclaim
thy being and thy ways.

Not for the lip of praise alone
nor even the praising heart
I ask, but for a life made up
of praise in every part:

Praise in the common things of life
its goings out and in;
praise in each duty and each deed,
however small and mean.

Fill every part of me with praise:
let all my being speak
of thee and of thy love, O Lord,
poor though I be and weak.

So shall no part of day or night
from sacredness be free;
but all my life, in every step,
be fellowship with thee.   *Horatius Bonar, 1808-89*

The Word of God

PSALM 67

Know that the Lord is God, ▪
we are his people and the sheep of his pasture.

1 God be gracious to us and bless us ▪
   and make your face to shine upon us,
2 That your way may be known upon earth, ▪
   your saving power among all nations.
3 Let the peoples praise you, O God; ▪
   let all the peoples praise you.
4 O let the nations rejoice and be glad, ▪
   for you will judge the peoples righteously
      and govern the nations upon earth.
5 Let the peoples praise you, O God; ▪
   let all the peoples praise you.
6 Then will the earth bring forth her increase, ▪
   and God, our own God, will bless us.
7 God shall bless us, ▪
   and all the ends of the earth will fear him.

A BIBLE READING

VISION OF THE HOLY CITY

Monday	*Revelation 21: 1-4*
Tuesday	*Revelation 21: 5-14*
Wednesday	*Revelation 21: 15-22*

or

Jesus answered Judas (not Judas Isacariot), saying, 'Those who love me will keep my word, and my Father will love them, and we will come to them and make our home with them. Whoever does not love me does not keep my words; and the word that you hear is not mine, but is from the Father who sent me.

'I have said these things to you while I am still with you. But the Advocate, the Holy Spirit, whom the Father will send in my name, will teach you everything, and remind you of all that I have said to you. Peace I leave with you; my peace I give to you. I do not give to you as the world gives. Do not let your hearts be troubled, and do not let them be afraid. You heard me say to you, "I am going away, and I am coming to you." If you loved me, you would rejoice that I am going to the Father, because the Father is greater than I. And now I have told you this before it occurs, so that when it does occur, you may believe.' *John 14: 23-29*

A CANTICLE

NUNC DIMITTIS
Luke 2: 29-32

1 Now, Lord, you let your servant go in peace; ▪
   your word has been fulfilled.
2 My own eyes have seen the salvation ▪
   which you have prepared in the sight of every people.

Sixth Week of Easter

3 A light to reveal you to the nations, ▪
and the glory of your people Israel.

Prayer

INTERCESSIONS AND THANKSGIVINGS

Pray for grace and strength
  to keep the commandments of Jesus.
Pray at this time for all those whose work
  sets food on our tables, and for all in need.
Pray for the work of all agencies
  which seek to alleviate hunger and distress
  in the face of natural and man-made disasters.
Give thanks for insights granted to men and women
  which have enriched human life,
  especially in the fields of agriculture and medicine.
Give thanks for all dedicated service to the poor and weak.

THE COLLECT OF EASTER 6

God our redeemer,
you have delivered us from the power of darkness
and brought us into the kingdom of your Son:
Grant, that as by his death he has recalled us to life
so by his continual presence in us
he may raise us to eternal joy;
through Jesus Christ our Lord. Amen.

or one of these prayers
O God,
you have promised to make your dwelling place
within the hearts of all who hear your words
and put them into practice.
Send your Spirit to bring to our mind
all that your Son did and taught,
and empower us to bear witness to him
in our own words and deeds.
We ask this through our Lord Jesus Christ, your Son,
who lives and reigns with you
in the unity of the Holy Spirit,
one God for ever and ever. Amen.

Uniting in Prayer II

Loving God,
you make your home with your people;
may the Spirit arouse the love of Christ among us,
that we may do your will and find your peace
in Jesus' name. Amen. *Uniting in Prayer II*

THE LORD'S PRAYER

AN ENDING

Into your hands, O Lord, I commend my spirit;
   for you have redeemed me, O Lord God of truth.
Keep me as the apple of your eye;
   hide me under the shadow of your wings.
In righteousness shall I see you;
   your presence will give me joy.

The Ascension Day

Preparation

A SENTENCE OF SCRIPTURE

Since we have a great high priest, Jesus, the Son of God, let us boldly approach the throne of grace, so that we may receive mercy and find grace to help in time of need.
Hebrews 4: 14, 16

A PRAYER OF PENITENCE

Call to mind your sins of commission and omission, and bow before the ascended Lord.
Have mercy on us, O God, the Almighty,
Jesus Christ, Son of the living God;
Eternal Judge, have mercy.
Royal abundant Lord,
Great God, to whom we pray,
have mercy,
for it is your very nature to have mercy and to forgive;
thanks be to God.

HYMN

Where high the heavenly temple stands,
the house of God not made with hands,
a great High Priest our nature wears,
the Guardian of mankind appears.

He, who for men their surety stood,
and poured on earth his precious Blood,
pursues in heaven his mighty plan,
the Saviour and the Friend of man.

Though now ascended up on high,
he bends on earth a brother
partaker of the human name,
he knows the frailty of our frame.

In every pang that rends the heart
the Man of sorrows had a part;
he sympathizes with our grief,
and to the sufferer sends relief.

With boldness, therefore, at the throne
let us make all our sorrows known,
and ask the aid of heavenly power
to help us in the evil hour.

Michael Bruce, 1746-67

The Word of God

PSALM 93

God has gone up with a merry noise, ■
the Lord with the sound of the trumpet. Alleluia.

1 The Lord is king and has put on glorious apparel; ■
 the Lord has put on his glory
  and girded himself with strength.
2 He has made the whole world so sure ■
 that it cannot be moved.
3 Your throne has been established from of old; ■
 you are from everlasting.
4 The floods have lifted up, O Lord,
  the floods have lifted up their voice; ■
 the floods lift up their pounding waves.
5 Mightier than the thunder of many waters,
  mightier than the breakers of the sea, ■
 the Lord on high is mightier.
6 Your testimonies are very sure; ■
 holiness adorns your house, O Lord, for ever.

Ascension Day

A BIBLE READING

Jesus said to his disciples, 'These are my words that I spoke to you while I was still with you – that everything written about me in the law of Moses, the prophets, and the psalms must be fulfilled.' Then he opened their minds to understand the scriptures, and he said to them, 'Thus it is written, that the Messiah is to suffer and to rise from the dead on the third day, and that repentance and forgiveness of sins is to be proclaimed in his name to all nations, beginning from Jerusalem. You are witnesses of these things. And see, I am sending upon you what my Father promised; so stay here in the city until you have been clothed with power from on high.'

Then he led them out as far as Bethany, and, lifting up his hands, he blessed them. While he was blessing them, he withdrew from them and was carried up into heaven. And they worshipped him, and returned to Jerusalem with great joy; and they were continually in the temple blessing God. *Luke 24: 44-53*

A CANTICLE

TE DEUM Part 1
1. We praise you, O God ▪
   we acclaim you as the Lord;
2. All creation worships you ▪
   the Father everlasting.
3. To you all angels, all the powers of heaven ▪
   the cherubim and seraphim, sing in endless praise,
4. Holy, holy, holy Lord, God of power and might ▪
   heaven and earth are full of your glory.

5 The glorious company of apostles praise you ▪
   the noble fellowship of prophets praise you.
6 The white-robed army of martyrs praise you ▪
   throughout the world, the holy Church acclaims you.
7 Father, of majesty unbounded ▪
   your true and only Son, worthy of all praise,
   the Holy Spirit, advocate and guide.

Prayer

INTERCESSIONS AND THANKSGIVINGS

Pray for the nations of the world and their leaders,
   for peace and the reconciliation of all where differences
   divide men and women.
Give thanks for the apostolic gospel committed to the
   Church,
   for all works of compassion
   and for every service that proclaims God's love.

THE COLLECT OF THE DAY

Grant, we pray, Almighty God,
that as we believe your only-begotten Son
our Lord Jesus Christ
to have ascended into the heavens;
So we in heart and mind may also ascend
and with him continually dwell;
who is alive and reigns with you and the Holy Spirit,
one God, now and for ever. Amen.

Ascension Day

or one of these prayers:
Eternal Father,
reaching from end to end of the universe
and ordering all things with your mighty arm:
for you, time is the unfolding of truth that already is,
the unveiling of beauty that is yet to be.
Your Son has saved us in history
   by rising from the dead,
so that, transcending time,
he might free us from death.
May his presence among us
   lead to the vision of unlimited truth
and unfold the beauty of your love;
through Christ our Lord. Amen.

Uniting in Prayer II

Jesus Christ,
you left your disciples
   only that you might send the Holy Spirit.
Grant us the Spirit of truth
to convince the world
that you are risen from the dead
and that to you all knees shall bow,
to the glory of God the Father. Amen.

THE LORD'S PRAYER

AN ENDING

Christ has opened the gate of glory;
Christ prays for us at the right hand of the Father.
Christ descended to lift us up to be with him.
Alleluia!

Days between the Ascension Day and Pentecost

Preparation

A SENTENCE OF SCRIPTURE

The Lord is king! Let the earth rejoice; let the multitude of the isles be glad! *Psalm 97: 1*

A PRAYER OF PENITENCE

We have not always worshipped God our Creator.
Lord, have mercy.

We have not always followed Christ our Saviour.
Christ, have mercy.

We have not always trusted in the Holy Spirit, our Guide.
You are sent to be with us for ever.
Lord, have mercy. *New Patterns*

HYMN

Conquering kings their titles take
from the foes they captive make;
Jesus, by a nobler deed,
from the thousands he hath freed.

Yes, none other name is given
unto mortals under heaven,
which can make the dead arise,
and exalt them to the skies.

That which Christ so hardly wrought,
that which he so dearly bought,
that salvation, brethren, say,
shall we madly cast away?

Rather, gladly for that Name
bear the Cross, endure the shame;
joyfully for him to die
is not death, but victory.

Jesu, who dost condescend
to be called the sinner's Friend,
hear us, as to thee we pray,
glorying in thy Name today.

Glory to the Father be,
glory, holy Son, to thee,
glory to the Holy Ghost,
from the saints and angel-host. *18th century Latin*

The Word of God

PSALM 97: 1-6

God is king of all the earth. ■
sing praises with all your skill. Alleluia.

1 The Lord is king: let the earth rejoice; ■
   let the multitude of the isles be glad.
2 Clouds and darkness are round about him; ■
   righteousness and justice
      are the foundation of his throne.
3 Fire goes before him ■
   and burns up his enemies on every side.
4 His lightnings lit up the world; ■
   the earth saw it and trembled.
5 The mountains melted like wax
      at the presence of the Lord, ■
   at the presence of the Lord of the whole earth.
6 The heavens declared his righteousness, ■
   and all the peoples have seen his glory.

A BIBLE READING

Friday after the Ascension Day	*Exodus 33: 12-17*
Saturday after the Ascension Day	*Exodus 33: 18-23*
Monday	*Exodus 40: 16-38*
Tuesday	*2 Chronicles 5: 2-14*
Wednesday	*Luke 9: 18-27*
Thursday	*Galatians 5: 16-25*
Friday	*Galatians 6: 7-10*
Saturday	*Luke 1: 26-38*

or

Jesus continued in prayer to his Father, looking up to heaven and saying:

'Father, I ask not only on behalf of these whom you gave me, but also on behalf of those who will believe in me through their word, that they may all be one. As you, Father, are in me and I am in you, may they also be in us, so that the world may believe that you have sent me. The glory that you have given me I have given them, so that they may be one, as we are one, I in them and you in me, that they may become completely one, so that the world may know that you have sent me and have loved them even as you have loved me. Father, I desire that those also, whom you have given me, may be with me where I am, to see my glory, which you have given me because you loved me before the foundation of the world.

'Righteous Father, the world does not know you, but I know you; and these know that you have sent me. I made your name known to them, and I will make it known, so that the love with which you have loved me may be in them, and I in them.' *John 17: 20-26*

Days between Ascension and Pentecost

A SONG OF CHRIST'S GLORY
Philippians 2: 5-11

1. Christ Jesus was in the form of God; ■
   but he did not cling to equality with God.
2. He emptied himself, taking the form of a servant ■
   and was born in our human likeness.
3. And being found in human form
      he humbled himself ■
   and became obedient unto death
      even death on a cross.
4. Therefore God has highly exalted him: ■
   and bestowed on him the name above every name.
5. That at the name of Jesus every knee should bow: ■
   in heaven and on earth and under the earth.
6. And every tongue confess that Jesus Christ is Lord: ■
   to the glory of God the Father.

Prayer

INTERCESSIONS AND THANKSGIVINGS

Pray in these nine days
   for the renewal of the Church by the power of the Holy Spirit,
   for that unity of the church for which Christ prayed and by the means he shall choose,
   for renewed obedience to the Great Commission to preach the Gospel to all the world.
Give thanks for the heritage we have received from the times of the apostles,
   for the mission in which God has called us to share,
   for the will to unity, and its fruit in common action.

THE COLLECT OF EASTER 7

O God the King of Glory,
you have exalted your only Son Jesus Christ
with great triumph to your kingdom in heaven:
Mercifully give us faith to know
that, as he promised,
he abides with us on earth to the end of time;
who is alive and reigns with you and the Holy Spirit,
one God, now and for ever. Amen.

or one of these prayers:
Risen ascended Lord,
as we rejoice at your triumph,
fill your Church on earth with power and compassion,
that all who are estranged by sin
may find forgiveness and know your peace,
to the glory of God the Father. Amen.

Alternative Collects

God, our creator and redeemer,
your Son Jesus prayed that his followers might be one.
Make all Christians one with him,
as he is one with you,
so that in peace and concord
we may carry to the world the message of your love;
through Jesus Christ our Lord,
who lives and reigns with you and the Holy Spirit,
one God, now and for ever. Amen.

Uniting in Prayer II

Days between Ascension and Pentecost

THE LORD'S PRAYER

AN ENDING

To God, who by the power at work within us,
is able to do far more abundantly
than all we ask or think,
to him be glory in the Church and in Christ Jesus
to all generations for ever and ever. Amen.

Ephesians 3: 20

The Day of Pentecost

Preparation

A SENTENCE OF SCRIPTURE

When the Comforter comes, he will prove the world wrong about sin and righteousness and judgment: about sin, because they do not believe in me; about righteousness, because I am going to the Father and you will see me no longer; about judgment, because the ruler of this world has been condemned. *John 16: 8-11*

A PRAYER OF PENITENCE

We have wounded your love.
O God, heal us.

We stumble in darkness:
Light of the world transfigure us.

We forget that we are your home,
Spirit of God, dwell in us.

Living God,
in whom we live and move and have our being,
all that we are, have been and shall be is known to you,
to the inner secrets of our hearts
and all that rises to trouble us.
Living flame, burn into us,
cleansing wind, blow through us,
fountain of water rise up within us,
forgiving and enabling us to love
    and praise in deed and truth.

Prayer Book of New Zealand altd

HYMN

Come, Holy Spirit, heavenly Dove,
with light and comfort from above;
be thou our Guardian, thou our Guide;
o'er every thought and step preside.

The light of truth to us display,
and make us know and choose thy way;
plant holy fear in every heart,
that we from God may n'er depart.

Lead us to Christ, the living Way,
nor let us from his pastures stray;
lead us to holiness, the road
that we must take to dwell with God.

Lead us to heaven, that we may share
fulness of joy for ever there;
lead us to God, our final rest,
to be with him for ever blest.

Simon Browne, 1680-1732

The Word of God

PSALM 139: 1-11

Send your Holy Spirit ▪
and clothe us with power from on high. Alleluia.

1 O Lord, you have searched me out and known me; ▪
   you know my sitting down and my rising up;
     you discern my thoughts from afar.
2 You mark out my journeys and my resting place ▪
   and are acquainted with all my ways.
3 For there is not a word on my tongue, ▪
   but you, O Lord, know it altogether.

The Day of Pentecost

4 You encompass me behind and before ▪
 and lay your hand upon me.
5 Such knowledge is too wonderful for me, ▪
 so high that I cannot attain it.
6 Where can I go then from your spirit? ▪
 Or where can I flee from your presence?
7 If I climb up to heaven, you are there; ▪
 if I make the grave my bed, you are there also.
8 If I take the wings of the morning ▪
 and dwell in the uttermost parts of the sea,
9 Even there your hand shall lead me, ▪
 your right hand hold me fast.
10 If I say, 'Surely the darkness will cover me ▪
 and the light around me turn to night,'
11 Even darkness is no darkness with you;
 the night is as clear as the day; ▪
 darkness and light to you are both alike.

A BIBLE READING

Philip said to Jesus, 'Lord, show us the Father, and we will be satisfied.' Jesus said to him, 'Have I been with you all this time, Philip, and you still do not know me? Whoever has seen me has seen the Father. How can you say, "Show us the Father"? Do you not believe that I am in the Father and the Father is in me? The words that I say to you I do not speak on my own; but the Father who dwells in me does his works. Believe me that I am in the Father and the Father is in me; but if you do not, then believe me because of the works themselves. Very truly, I tell you, the one who believes in me will also do the works that I do and, in fact, will do greater works than these, because I am going to the Father. I will do whatever you ask in my name, so that the Father may be glorified in the Son. If in my name you ask me for anything, I will do it.

'If you love me, you will keep my commandments. And I will ask the Father, and he will give you another Advocate, to be with you for ever. This is the Spirit of truth, whom the world cannot receive, because it neither sees him nor knows him. You know him, because he abides with you, and he will be in you.'

John 14: 8-17

A CANTICLE

GREAT AND WONDERFUL
Revelation 15: 3, 4 and 7: 10, 12

1 Great and wonderful are your deeds
    Lord God, the Almighty, ∎
  just and true are your ways, O King of the nations.
2 Who shall not revere and praise your name, O Lord ∎
  for you alone are holy.
3 All nations shall come and worship in your presence ∎
  for your just dealings have been revealed.
4 To him who sits on the throne, and to the Lamb ∎
  be praise and honour, glory and might,
  for ever and ever. Amen.

Prayer

INTERCESSIONS AND THANKSGIVINGS

Pray that the Church worldwide recover its sense of mission;
   for the unity of all who are called and inspired by the
   One Spirit,
      and for all who do not know the fulness of life that is
      God's will.
Give thanks for the Spirit whose working transforms the life
   of the Church
      and the signs of his work in the transformation of the
      lives of individuals.

THE COLLECT OF PENTECOST

Almighty God,
who on the day of Pentecost
sent your Holy Spirit to the apostles
with the wind from heaven and in tongues of flame,
filling them with joy
and boldness to preach the gospel:
By the power of the same Spirit
strengthen us to witness to your truth
and to draw everyone to the fire of your love;
through Jesus Christ our Lord. Amen.

or one of these prayers:
Living God,
you breathe life into us
   and your Spirit is the breath of life for the Church.
Renew us with the Spirit,
transform us with your truth
and give us ability to share
   the Good News of Jesus with power.
We ask this in his name. Amen.   *Uniting in Christ II*

Spirit of the living God,
give fire to our faith,
breathe new life into our prayer
and give us new power to witness
to the love of the God and Father
   of our Lord Jesus Christ.

THE LORD'S PRAYER

AN ENDING

The Spirit of truth lead us into all truth,
give us grace to confess that Jesus is Lord
and to proclaim the word and works of God. Amen.

Acknowledgements

Texts are reproduced with the permission of the copyright owners from:

The Book of Common Prayer of the Church of Ireland (Revision of 2004) © 2004 Representative Church Body, Church of Ireland House, Dublin 6.

Bible passages are from the *New Revised Standard Version*, Anglicized edition. © 1989, 1995 by the Division of Christian Education of the National Council of Churches of Christ in the USA, and are used by permission. All rights reserved.

Sentences indicated by TNIV are from *Today's New International Version* (TNIV) © 2002 by the International Bible Society. Used by permission of Hodder and Stoughton Publishers. All rights reserved.

Psalms are from the Psalter in *Common Worship: Services and Prayers for the Church of England* © 2000 by Archbishops' Council.
Several of the prayers alternative to the collect are also from *Common Worship: Alternative Collects* © 2004.
Some canticles and prayers are from *Common Worship: Daily Prayer* © 2005 by the Archbishops' Council.

The canticles, *Te Deum* and *Nunc Dimittis* are © 1988 English Language Liturgical Consultation (ELLC).

Some prayers are from:
A New Zealand Prayer Book © 1988 The Church of the Province of New Zealand.
Uniting in Worship II © 2005 The Uniting Church of Australia.

Lutheran Renewal Worship and Sundays and Seasons © 2004 Fortress Press

Revised Common Lectionary Prayers ©2002 Consultation on Common Texts.

Bible citations from *Revised Common Lectionary Daily Readings* ©Consultation on Common Texts. Used by permission.

Other texts are by the compiler. If, through inadvertence, copyright material has been used without permission or acknowledgement the publisher will be grateful to be informed and will make the necessary correction in a subsequent edition.